IMAGES
of Canada

SAINT JOHN

Cornelius Sparrow came to Saint John as an escaped slave in 1851. By 1862 he owned the Royal Saloon on Charlotte Street (the alley next to Shoppers Drug Mart on Charlotte was known as Sparrow's Alley). The Royal sold fruit, vegetables, and oysters, and was a ladies and gents hair dressing salon. In 1874 Cornelius moved to Germain Street and operated the Victoria Dining Saloon until its destruction in the Great Fire of 1877. After re-opening, Cornelius stayed in business until 1883, when he began work as a waiter. (PIRP #3191.)

Harold E. Wright

First published 1996
Copyright © Harold E. Wright, 1996

ISBN 0-7524-0463-6

Published by Arcadia Publishing,
an imprint of the Chalford Publishing Corporation
One Washington Center, Dover, New Hampshire 03820
Printed in Great Britain

Library of Congress Cataloging-in-Publication Data applied for

Contents

Acknowledgments		6
Saint John: 1863-1974		7
1.	Streetscapes	9
2.	Leisure	15
3.	Police and Fire Departments	23
4.	Women at Work	31
5.	Domestic Architecture	37
6.	Public Spaces	45
7.	Militia Artillery	49
8.	Marching Bands	55
9.	Harbour	59
10.	Partridge Island	69
11.	Celebrations	75
12.	Shipbuilding	85
13.	Transportation	89
14.	Schools and Churches	95
15.	Sports	103
16.	Public Buildings	107
17.	Businesses	115
18.	The Saint John General Hospital	127

Acknowledgments

This book has been a collaboration of many people. I thank the following: Arthur Doyle, former publisher of the *Evening Times Globe*, who suggested a book of photos back in 1991; the staff at the Information Centre of the Public Library and the Archives of the N.B. Museum; David Goss, Fred Miller, Rob Roy, Bob Elliot, Jim Bezanson, John McLean, Bobby Donovan, Linda Nickerson, Trina Young, and Rick Smith; the many friends and acquaintances who shared photographs with me; the readers of my weekly "Historic Saint John" column in the *Times Globe*; and most important, my wife Cheryl, whose understanding and support make all this effort worthwhile.

The photographs document Saint John from 1863 to 1974. Sometimes a circa date is used—indicating that the precise date proved impossible to determine, but should lie within five years of the year stated. The abbreviations used in the photograph credits are as follows: NAC—National Archives Canada; PANB—Provincial Archives New Brunswick; PIRP—Partridge Island Research Project; and SJPC—Saint John Port Corporation. If I have inadvertently omitted somebody, my apologies. Only I am responsible for any errors of fact.

I dedicate this volume to our son Jason. Although he is only four years old this month, Cheryl and I both hope that he will learn about and appreciate his city through reading this book—although he may not be able to read it for another few years.

Harold E. Wright
June 1996

Saint John: 1863-1974

The decades immediately following the mid-nineteenth century have been labelled by many historians as Saint John's "golden age." At that time we were the fourth largest shipbuilding centre in the world, launching an average of two ships every week.

The architecture of the city from that era testifies to the nature of the area's economy. An article concerning Saint John's architecture, published in the *Daily Telegraph* in the 1850s, said that "utility moreso than ornament determined a building's style and form and that a city may go on with such structures for a half century or more without anyone endeavouring to break its monotony by the erection of structures of a more tasteful character."

On June 20, 1877, a fire erupted at York Point and burned out of control for nine hours, destroying the business and residential heart of the city. This fire could well have meant the doom of Saint John, but architects, engineers, masons, carpenters, and labourers came from all over the continent to aid in the rebuilding of the city. The prophecy that "From these very ashes and ruins a brighter, a more glorious and more prosperous city will arise" came true, for within five years the city was rebuilt.

Many businessmen used this opportunity to shift their capital from shipping to banking, land transportation, merchandising, and other land-based service industries. In the 1880s and 1890s, Saint John's industrial capital, employment, and industrial output increased. In 1882 Mr. P.R. Edictor, in an address to the Ladies Society of the Congregational Church, speculated that in fifty years time Saint John would have a population of 468,000 people. He said that various carrying lines would be inaugurated to transport people to and from work and places of leisure. There would be a rapid-transit double-tracked elevated railway skirting the south end and the one harbour ferry would be expanded to three. He also predicted that "rum and intemperance have now for many years been unknown evils, and the jail is the most rickety, unused building in the city, while the police are getting rich in peaceful avocations."

The city rested its economic hopes on the continuing prosperity on the port. The Canadian government at this point was using Portland, Maine, as the Canadian winter port. In 1894 two members of Parliament from Saint John threatened to resign, provided the incentive for the federal government to provide a $25,000 subsidy to the Beaver Line steamships to use Saint John during the winter. In 1896 Ottawa stopped using Portland and directed traffic to Saint John.

Over the next twenty-plus years harbour facilities improved and were expanded. Port activities were described in the following manner: ". . . the waterfront was not a pretty place, but it was busy, where ships from all over the world came to load and unload in the winter port . . . [and the] Saint John longshoremen were more honest than those anywhere else, and more efficient."

Peacetime port activity was supplemented during World War I when the port assumed a major military role. As the major industrial centre in the Maritimes, and an ice-free port, ships carried munitions, food stuffs, horses, machinery, and troops overseas. Over twenty thousand

New Brunswickers flocked to the recruiting stations to "Fight for the Empire." At home, women, fuelled by the spark of patriotism, replaced men in the factories.

The end of the war coupled with the disastrous effects of the depression of the 1930s brought economic hardships to the city. On the brink of economic disaster, the city sold the harbour facilities to the federal government in 1927, and not a moment too soon. In 1931 most of the west side dock facility burned. Quick federal aid to rebuild the port saved the city's economy. Another federal relief project was the construction of the municipal airport in Millidgeville. We could now service national and international customers by land, sea, and air. The recently constructed drydock allowed us to compete nationally for ship repair and construction projects.

The outbreak of World War II again brought economic prosperity, but also the threat of attack from a European enemy. Fear of German submarine and air attacks was so great that several forts were established around the harbour rim. The financial benefits generated by the war greatly overshadowed this threat of attack.

The 1950s and 1960s saw many changes in the physical appearance of Saint John. Wartime housing was built in the Rifle Range and Portland Place, and suburbs emerged in Forest Hills, Champlain Heights, and Millidgeville. The Fairview Plaza and Simpson Sears opened, as did the Lancaster Mall. The oil refinery opened. A massive urban renewal program replaced slum housing and tenements on Main Street and in the East End. These wooden buildings were replaced by concrete office buildings, highways, landscaped areas, and shopping malls.

The 1970s was the end of an era for many familiar landmarks. The old city hall on Prince William Street closed as our municipal government moved into a new city hall. Construction began or was finished at the Simonds and Millidgeville North high schools, the Brunterm container terminal at the port, and the Point Lepreau nuclear power station. The Bricklin came and went. The old Kirk in Carleton was destroyed by fire. The General Hospital was to be phased out. The Union Station was closed and then demolished. MRA's and the Royal Hotel were closed and demolished for the Brunswick Square complex. By mid-decade, the physical landscape of our city had been irreversibly changed.

One
Streetscapes

Carmarthen Street, facing north to the Cathedral, has certainly changed since c. 1865. C.F. Munroe & Co. on Union Street offered hay, oats and corn, and groceries. The Cathedral, which dominates the skyline, is without its spire, added in 1871. The two Greek Revival homes at the right are across from the Old Public Burial Ground. Note the dirt street, and the gas lamps at the corners of Elliott Row and Union Street. (Courtesy NAC.)

To commemorate the centennial of the Loyalists in 1883, the Women's Christian Temperance Union placed this fountain in King's Square. It was taken down in 1963. Stoerger's Studio was on the second floor of 75 Charlotte Street (left). The first floor was occupied by D.O.L. Warlock, a jeweller, optician, and watchmaker. Across the street was E.G. Nelson & Co., importers and dealers in books, stationery, fancy goods, Kodak cameras, and photographic supplies. (Courtesy PANB.)

Market Square changed little from the post-1877 fire period to the 1960s. In 1918 there was MRA's furniture store, where brass and iron beds, mattresses, and springs were advertised on fascia signs. Next door was Malcolm Mackay [lumber] Limited, the Confederation Life Association, and the Union Bank of Canada. W.H. Thorne & Co. Ltd. (advertising nets, lines and twines, athletic and sporting goods, and hardware) was across the street, as was Cowie & Edwards (fire and marine insurance and average adjusters). (Lynch Coll., PIRP #6822.)

Prince William Street, shown here in 1918. The post office, built in the Neoclassical Revival style, opened in 1914. The Seamen's Institute, founded in 1893, provided spiritual and social guidance for mariners. This building was erected in 1908, with an auditorium, offices, and kitchen on the ground floor, and offices, accommodation, recreation rooms, showers, and baths on the upper floors. In 1943 alone the Institute assisted over 58,000 mariners. (Lynch Coll., PIRP #6824.)

Prince Edward Street used to be known as Brussell's Street, but was renamed at the time of World War I. This section was close to the intersection with Waterloo Street. Frank Marney operated a saw filing service from 511–12 Brussell's Street. Harry L. McAlary was a watchmaker and jeweller at 55 Brussells. Next to McAlary was a barbershop. The car at the left is a 1947 Chevy, and the Irving Oil truck is a 1947 International. (Condon Coll., PIRP #5973.)

After the Great 1877 Fire, King Street East developed as one of the most desirable areas of the city to live. Originally known as Great Georges Street, there was a military blockhouse at the intersection with Wentworth. The second building at the right was built for Carson Flood in 1878. Designed by Henry P. Clark and John L. Briggs, it was described in an 1878 issue of the *American Architect and Building News*. Flood, who sold pianos and organs, went bankrupt about six months after the article appeared. Sold at auction in 1879, the unfinished house sold for $2,425. This photograph dates from the early 1950s. (PIRP #501.)

Prince Edward Street in the 1950s was enjoying its last years as a community. By the mid-1960s the entire East End was demolished and redeveloped for malls, office buildings, and some housing. The four Chevy taxis are in front of a store; across the street is a fish and chip shop. (Condon Coll., PIRP #5970.)

Market Street had seen many changes by the time this c. 1952 photograph was taken. The streetcar tracks had been removed, replaced by City Transit buses. The cannon in the square had been melted down, and the buildings showed signs of their age. Horton & Walsh was still here, although MRA's have been replaced by Emerson-Wheaton, and the Sherwin-Williams paint store is next to the Canada Permanent building. The restaurants, clothing stores, second-hand shops, and hardware supply stores on Dock Street would remain until fire and urban renewal removed them in the 1950s–1970s. (PIRP #3647.)

In June 1955, the City Works department undertook a major resurfacing of uptown streets. It took two days to put a one-inch layer of asphalt on the street, the crews taking advantage of the warm, dry weather. King Street was one of the last to be done; the cost of doing just King was $2,755. To lessen the impact on uptown traffic as much as possible, repaving crews also worked at night. (PIRP #3204.)

Rothesay and Thorne Avenues, as seen from the roof of the General Hospital, reveal a streetscape that has completely changed. The Beatty Washer building in the lower left is one of the few remaining—it is now Universal Sales Ltd. The new post office replaced many of the buildings at the left centre, and the old City Works building on Rothesay Avenue was replaced by new facilities in the 1980s. McAvity's is gone, although when this photograph was taken in 1951, Fred J. Esson had yet to get stuck on the smokestack, as he did in 1954. The hills behind McAvity's became Forest Hills, and at the far right the old East End grounds, used by the military during the war, was redeveloped for the Dominion and Canadian tire stores. (James Coll., PIRP #4455.)

Two
Leisure

Simeon Jones, a brewer and former mayor of Saint John, was considered one of the wealthiest men in Canada when this c. 1885 photograph was taken of his children. Perhaps they each owned their own bike, or were members of the Saint John Bicycle Club. From left to right are: Ernest (killed in action during World War I), Fred C. (died in service during World War I), Edna (married and moved to the UK), Robert Keltie, Katherine (married and moved to the UK), George West (manager of the York Cotton Mill), Simeon Jr., and Andrew. (Jones Coll., PIRP #5896.)

The Miller family was long involved with lumbering and sawmill operations in Saint John. Here the family has gathered at Pokiok, c. 1900, for a picnic. (Fawcett Coll., PIRP #578.)

The Dufferin Hotel was one of the many fine hotels in the city. Renovated in 1895, it boasted certified sanitation, splendid baths, excellent cuisine, and private grounds for promenade garden concerts twice a week. In this 1909 photograph are: John Boyd (manager), John McCormick (wine clerk), Joseph McCarthy (coachman), James H. Doody (steamfitter), Albert L. Foster (treasurer, Simms & Co.), Billie Ward, and Jack O'Neil. (PIRP #6042.)

A group of men, probably members of an informal "Men Only" club, strike a casual pose for a photograph. Perhaps they enjoyed girl watching, evident from the "Women Only" photographs on the wall. This *c.* 1910 photograph was probably taken by Vance Pender, son of James Pender of the Pender nail works. (Dexter Coll., PIRP #4323.)

These ladies, probably members of a church organization, are fishing with what we would today call the bare necessities. They have no rubber boots, and two of the ladies are using switches as poles. Perhaps the lady on the left has caught a fish using a pole manufactured by Joseph Dalzell, a well-known maker of fishing poles from 1900 to the 1920s. (Lt Col. GGK Holder Coll., PIRP #5959.)

The Junior Band of St. Phillip's African Methodist Church is shown here at the corner of Queen and Pitt Streets, c. 1920. The church was organized in 1861 and met here until 1940. Posing for this photo are: Percey Johnson, Thema Ritchie, Rev. Claude Stewart and his daughter, and members of the Leslie, Scott, and Hogan families. When the church was demolished city officials feared that buildings "to house colored people will be erected thereon, an undesirable possibility for this location." (Skinner Coll., PIRP #3577.)

Playing in the snow is always more fun when you have family and friends around. In the backyard of their home at 114 Douglas Avenue, Harriet J. Roberts joined Blanche Tapley and Sally F. Roberts in building igloos during a winter in the 1920s. Perhaps the flag and snowshoes made for a more realistic North Pole scenario. (Roberts Coll., PIRP #2310.)

There were many popular theatrical and musical performers; one of the best known in both drama and music circles was Fred Joyce of West Saint John. From 1893 until his death in 1962, Fred was active with church choirs, and performed for the IODE, churches, the CNIB, and the Lancaster DVA. In March 1926 he directed and performed in the operetta *Lass of Limerick Town* at St. Patrick's Hall. Fred is at the centre rear wearing a white cap. His daughter Edna is seated at his right. Also on stage are: Josephine Owens (front, far left), Cyril Moore (back, ninth from the right), and Joe Moore (back, third from the right). In 1955 Fred received the Canadian Drama Award. (Joyce Coll., PIRP #7153.)

Many city streets were quickly converted to hills perfect for skiing or tobogganing after a snowfall. With less vehicular traffic after a c. 1935 storm, this group on Carmarthen Street is ready with their toboggan and skis. (Bormke Coll., PIRP #6720.)

The Strouds were west-siders, but chose Market Slip to have this c. 1937 photograph taken of their visiting relatives. Bill (left) is shown with his cousin Paul and Paul's wife Caroline, from San Francisco, and his mother, Bertha. Fred Stroud, Bill's father, probably took the photograph. (Stroud Coll., PIRP #456.)

Gerry Hanley worked for the National Drug Company and Pitfield Mackay from the 1940s until 1972. He moved to Douglas Avenue just before this photograph was taken in 1943. His family resided on the avenue until the New Brunswick Museum purchased their home and demolished it for a parking lot in the 1970s. His family, from left to right, included: Marilyn, Janet, Karen, his wife Marie, and David. Gerry served as a city councillor and deputy mayor from 1950 until 1971. (Hanley Coll., PIRP #2371.)

In 1950 Marilyn Hanley, like hundreds of other girls, joined Veronica Conway's dance and majorette group. Marilyn took baton, tap, and ballet lessons from Veronica for six years in the basement of St. Peter's Church. Recently Veronica happened to meet Marilyn after a break of close to fifty years. Marilyn must have been quite a student, for Veronica recognized her right away. (Hanley Coll., PIRP #2358.)

The fountain in the Old Public Burying Ground on Sydney Street was a favourite location for photographs. About 1950 Elaine and Patricia Atkinson left their home on Seaton Street, across the Marsh Creek, and came to the burial ground with their mother. They are posed on the fountain erected to commemorate the burial location of Dr. Nathan Smith. (Atkinson Coll., PIRP #5009.)

Although winter skating was great on an outdoor rink or at Lily Lake, the Main Street Forum remains in everybody's mind as "the" place to skate. These children are preparing for their skating pageant, c. 1955. The Forum burned down on March 20, 1967. (James Coll., PIRP #4469.)

Three
Police and Fire Departments

Constable Andy Duffy was "our natural born traffic officer." Andy stood at the head of King from 1920 to 1931 and again from 1938 until his death in 1940. "Everybody wanted to take Andy Duffy's picture. He was a great tourist attraction too. Everybody wanted to come and watch Andy direct the traffic." In August 1929 Lawrence Young, from Montreal, photographed Andy (left). (Young Coll., PIRP #3211.)

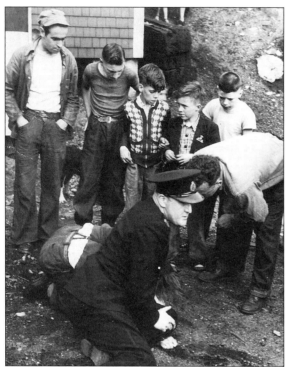

Shortly after joining the force in 1949, Constable Frank Shae apprehended this suspected felon, named London, at the foot of Simonds Street. This photograph won a newspaper award for the photographer, Lorne Pridham. The boy standing second from the left is Eddie Burbridge, who himself became a police officer. Frank served thirty years, retiring as a detective inspector. (Shae Coll., PIRP #7256.)

Detectives Frank Shae (left) and Tom McCormick (right) investigate the c. 1965 break-in at St. Peter's School. Shae recalled that there was a tremendous amount of damage done to the school. He also recalled Mayor Macaulay describing a policeman as "a longshoreman with a uniform." Both Shae and McCormick received their twenty-five-year service pin in 1974. McCormick retired in 1978, Shae in 1979. (McCormick Coll., PIRP #6666.)

Desk sergeant Leo Pye is shown here at the King Street East station. Leo joined the force in 1941 and retired in 1972. He served on Common Council from 1974 to 1989. After serving six months he wrote: "I have come to the conclusion that the laxity which exists in many . . . Departments can be attributed to the obvious reluctance of most Council members to rectify the existing inefficiencies." He died in 1989. (Pye Coll., PIRP #6008.)

The fire and police stations on King Street East were built in 1878. In 1953 a two-storey brick addition was made to the front of the police station, giving enlarged office space for the chief and deputy chief. Interior changes were made in an attempt to make the building more functional and comfortable for the police and inmates. In 1971 the police moved into the new city hall, and the old stations were demolished soon after. (PIRP #442.)

The Campanile or Bell Tower stood at the entrance to King's Square, at the head of King Street, from 1853 until it was destroyed in the Great 1877 fire. Designed by Matthew Stead to look like stone, but built of wood, this bell alarm was the second alarm bell located in the Square. It was designed to house a clock illuminated by gas, but this proved too costly. The arched wings were added in 1860 for the visit of the Prince of Wales. (Ferris Coll., PIRP #8128.)

No. 1 Salvage Corps & Fire Police was established in 1882 and moved into No. 3 station on Union Street in 1890. No. 2 Corps was formed in 1898 and was headquartered in No. 5 station on Main Street. Their principal job was to provide salvage and security to properties during and after a fire. Both corps amalgamated on the centennial of No. 1 in 1982. (Ferris Coll., PIRP #8058)

A well-dressed group of the Fairville firemen pose during Queen Victoria's Diamond Jubilee on June 22, 1897. "The Carleton firemen . . . their hosecart was trimmed . . . in tinsel and flowers. Her majesty's picture adorned a large mirror, . . . in the centre . . . was a miniature fountain which threw a tiny stream in the air, and a reflection was thrown on the mirror . . ." From left to right are: Joe Needley, George Fawcett, ? Clark, unknown, ? Harned, C. Sweet, A. Ring, Bill Christopher, Fred Ring, unknown, B. Fawcett, unknown, unknown, and ? McLeod. (Ferris. Coll., PIRP #8103.)

The men of No. 1 Hook & Ladder did a superb job of decorating their station on King Street East for the visit of the Duke and Duchess of Cornwall and York in 1901. Ladders run along the sides and the roof line of the building, with crossed axes held in place by rope. On the flag pole are crossed axes, a leather fire bucket, a lantern, a trumpet, and an illuminated box with portraits of the Royal couple. On the front of the building are buckets, lanterns, crossed axes, and fire hooks. Numerous flags adorn the building. (Ferris Coll., PIRP #8096.)

No. 1 Wellington Company, 211 Charlotte Street, was a volunteer company organized in 1851. The station, built in 1878, later became McLaughlin Tire in the 1950s. In 1907 a Grand Firemen's Tournament was held in September. Over one thousand firemen from the Maritimes and Maine participated in a parade, sports and firemen's competition, and concerts. No. 1 Hook & Ladder Company's float of the Rockwood Park Amusements won first prize. No. 1 Hose wagon and No. 1 Steamer are shown here. (Ferris Coll., PIRP #8039.)

No. 4 Portland station on City Road was built in early 1883 by Andrew Myles to a design by Francis Roden. In November 1964 the new No. 8 station went into service at Millidgeville and old No. 4 was demolished. Shown here c. 1940 are No. 3 Hook & Ladder and Pump No. #5, with John Cooper (left), Captain Lloyd Hayward, and C. Ryan (right). (Ferris Coll., PIRP #8062.)

No. 3 station, 156 Union Street, was built in 1890. No. 1 Salvage Corps & Fire Police were located here, as was the department's headquarters until the station was replaced by the new No. 1 station on Carmarthen Street in 1976. Shown here, c. 1950, are Pump No. 3 Reserve, Pump No. 3, and No. 1 Salvage Corps, with George Secord, Jack Spinny, Glen Neil, Dave Short, Captain John Ewart, and Percy Totten. (Ferris Coll., PIRP #8078.)

Members of the Lancaster Fire Department pose at No. 1 station, Church Avenue, c. 1953. The two drivers are Edmund "Bunger" Reid (left) and Fred Brownell (right). Ralph Kierstead is holding the Union Jack. (Kierstead Coll., PIRP #7243.)

A spectacular two-alarm fire on April 17, 1951, caused considerable damage to Green's Tobacco store. Constable Harry McKay sounded the first alarm at 10:20 am, and by noon the fire was under control. Green's was damaged by the fire, as were King Square Credit Jewellers' stockrooms and Alice Gray's Beauty Salon. There was smoke damage to McHarg's Beauty Salon on the second floor. Note the men examining the "Employment Bulletin" board at the right corner of the store, just behind the dump truck, while the others watch the fire, fearful that the rooftop Ganong sign will topple off the building. (Ferris Coll., PIRP #8117.)

Four
Women at Work

Annie C. Taylor joined NB Tel in 1900. "At the switchboard [sat] a long row of operators dressed in white shirtwaists, with balloon sleeves, and long black skirts. Each operator [wore] a black satin apron at the rear, rather than the front; this [was] to protect the skirt from becoming shiny on the leather seat of the chair." Annie was one of those operators. Her retirement in 1940 as toll chief operator was described "as though a corner stone had broken loose." (Courtesy Mary LeBlanc.)

World War I opened some non-traditional jobs for women. McAvity's foundry on Rothesay Avenue and its Brass Plant on Water Street employed a few hundred women over the course of the war. In a payroll ledger, kept by a man, are found the following comments: "She worked all right but her husband(?) was worthless . . . Stole the overalls issued her"; "thoroughly conscientious and a woman of high ideals"; "Latter part of her employment she lost interest . . . D.H. Mungall, our chemist, was interested. Married Mungall in September 1919"; "Lost weight to a big extent before I noticed & discovered that it was booze. Kept terrible hours and came to work soused & dirty;" "She and her sister have quite a reputation. One police court affair and a 'left town with a circus' episode." This is the Operation No. 10, Thread Mill Base, McAvity's 9.2-inch shell plant, Rothesay Avenue, 1918. (McAvity Coll., PIRP #7253.)

McAvity's chief inspector's office is shown here in 1918. (McAvity Coll., PIRP #7254.)

This view of the cafeteria in the 9.2-inch Shell Plant on Rothesay Avenue was taken in 1918. (McAvity Coll., PIRP #7255.)

In 1919 the office staff at James Robertson, a plumbing supplier at Lower Cove, continued the more traditional roles for their female employees. The three ladies appear to be secretaries. The only person identified is Cecil Herrington (second from the left). (Herrington Coll., PIRP, #5084.)

These women are packing paper tea bags on the second floor of the Red Rose Tea building. The two ladies at the left are "belt girls," with the ladies at the right being the "button girl" and the "box carrier." The box carrier kept the ladies supplied with boxes (in this case sixty-bag boxes). The belt carriers and button girl all packed tea. The button girl had the added responsibility of keeping the tea machine clear of clogged tea, the supply of paper bags replenished, and making sure that the cutting knife made clean cuts to the paper bags. Red Rose installed the first automated tea bag-filling machine in Canada. The ladies are, from left to right: Aggie Dayment, Rhoda Humphrey, Dorothy Ross, and Georgie Spragg, c. 1950 (Briggs Coll., PIRP #2270.)

The Red Rose coffee house on Chipman Hill was quite drafty, forcing employees to wear bandannas and coats in the spring and fall. The women are sorting coffee beans, c. 1940. (PIRP #4402.)

MRA's candy and cosmetic departments were located on the ground level. In this photograph, there are at least five female clerks behind the counters, and the majority of the shoppers are women, c. 1950. (PIRP #946.)

The York Cotton Mill opened in 1883 (a second mill was on Winter Street). In this c. 1955 image, the women are performing two tasks: on the left at least fifteen women are using sewing machines, while on the right, eight women are either measuring trouser legs, or cutting material. The cotton mill closed in 1958 and was demolished in 1994. (James Coll., PIRP #6103.)

Laura Foster was one of the first female hosts on CHSJ Television. She was on the air in the early 1960s to the mid-1970s, and hosted the current affairs show *Magazine on the Air*. Other female hosts were Jeanny Woods, on *It's Time for Juniors*, and Ann Ramey, on *Play Time with Miss Ann*. (Hebb Coll., PIRP #3865.)

Five
Domestic Architecture

Robert Jardine, a prominent grocer, built his home, Woodside, on the Great Marsh Road (Rothesay Avenue) before 1856. This house is a good example of the picturesque Carpenter Gothic style. Members of the Jardine family are in front, c. 1860, a few years before Robert's death. Notice the peacock just in front of the horse. The second-storey bay window and verandah have been removed, and the house is now a tenement. (Glen Coll., PIRP #898.)

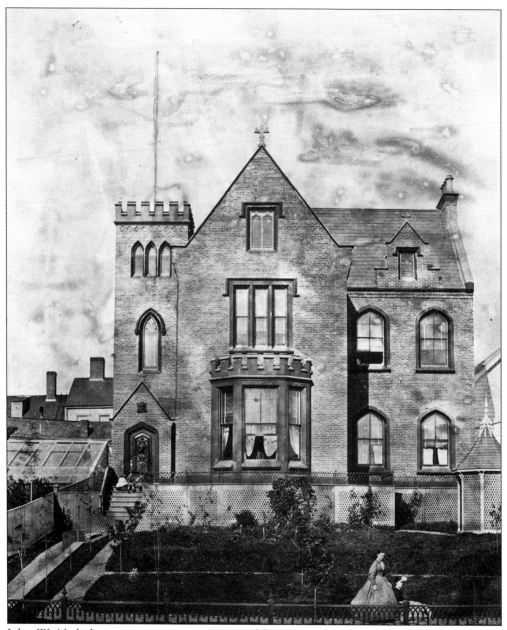

John W. Nicholson was a prominent wine and liquor merchant. His home on Mecklenburg Terrace in 1863 was of the Baronial Gothic style. The crenelated tower, ground-floor bay window, the gothic arch details in the cast-iron fence, and the gazebo at the right, created an image of wealth and prominence. Nicholson's home and business were destroyed in the Great

1877 Fire. He set up shop in the shanty town on King's Square and quickly hired William L. Prince, a carpenter and contractor, to build this new Second Empire home at 25 Mecklenburg Street. The tower and pressed metal tracery decorations are now missing, and the landscaping has changed, but Nicholson's home, now a tenement, still stands. (Major J.M. Grant Coll., PIRP #2440 and PIRP #3601.)

André Cushing, the man who gave us the first sulphite mill at the Reversible Falls, built his home, Keystone, on Lancaster Avenue in 1870–72. In 1872 he had Valentine Keillor, a Danish painter from Portland, Maine, decorate his home in *trompe l'oeil* paintings. The cornice in the dining room is a combination of this painting technique and 3-D dentils. The fireplace at the right was built as a fake, and the pass through into the kitchen is at the left. The original gas light fixtures, some with the heads of elk or deer, are still in place. The dining room has changed little since this *c.* 1890 photograph was taken. (PIRP #2817.)

The Edward L. Jewett home at 13 Queen Square is believed to have once been the manse for Trinity Church. One of the earlier occupants was Dr. John W. D. Gray, rector of both the Trinity and St. John's Churches. Jewett possibly bought the house after Grays death in 1868. It was a Greek Revival-style building, with balustrades at the roof edge, and a cast-iron newel post and fence on a sandstone wall. The house was destroyed in the Great Fire of 1877. (PIRP #6046.)

Senator John Boyd, of Daniel & Boyd, importer of British and foreign dry goods, was a successful merchant and politician who built his home, Ardencraig, at 19 Queen Square north after the Great 1877 Fire. During the 1901 visit of the Duke and Duchess of Cornwall and York, P. S. MacNutt, the owner at that time, allowed his home to be used by the Governor General. The drawing room reveals the opulence at the time for those with wealth. Note the beaded fan at the top of the doorway, and the ornate gas light fixture. By the 1950s this beautiful home had been converted into a rooming house. It was damaged by fire on December 31, 1965, and later demolished. (Dick Coll., PIRP #2391 and #2392.)

Fred Lord's home on Navy Island was seventy-five years old when this photograph was taken in 1930. Built of 3-inch deals on end, it was the oldest building on the island when it was demolished to allow for port expansion. There were eight families (forty-five people) left on the island when their property was expropriated. They all made their living from river and harbour fishing. (French Coll., PIRP #3119.)

William Peters, a leather and hide dealer, built this two-storey brick house at 190 King Street East, about 1880. James V. Russell, a prominent boot and shoe retailer with stores in the North and East Ends, bought the house in 1907. Russell eventually became one of the harbour commissionaires. His wife Elizabeth is the lady standing in the doorway just before World War I. (Chase Coll., PIRP #893.)

These two rooms of the Russell home show how busy a room can become with large pieces of furniture. Examine the fireplace, with its terra-cotta tiles around the opening, and the embossed iron liner. The fireplace mantle and mirror reveal the handsome woodwork still available from local industry. The brass bed in a second-floor bedroom is almost out of place with its simplicity. Note the sunburst beaded screen at the left, and the richness of detail in the wallpaper. Russell left the house to his daughter who rented it out. (Chase Coll., PIRP #896 and #892.)

Sherwood A. M. Skinner was a barrister living at 37 Mecklenburg Street in 1926. Several renovations related to lifestyle and decoration are evident here. Note the throw rugs on the hardwood floor. The fireplace is brick, creating a different atmosphere than the original one with a wood mantle. The light, hanging from an ornate plaster medallion, is an institutional fixture. Between the rooms are bi-folding French doors, popular in the late 1920s. (Edwards Coll., PIRP #4173.)

James Pender's sitting room, at 22 Queen Square, is shown here c. 1900. Pender was a prominent businessman, owning Pender's nail and wire company at Lower Cove. There are several pictures hanging from the picture rail on the wall. Photographs are literally just laying about on the radiator top, the organ, and on the pillow. The light fixture still appears to be gas. (Dexter Coll., PIRP #4330.)

Six
Public Spaces

King's Square is the symbolic centre of our city. Much has changed since this photograph was taken in 1930. Many of the buildings around the Admiral Beatty and Capitol Theatre have been demolished. At King Square north, Braegers and the Belmont Hotel disappeared by fire or demolition and were replaced by the Dominion Store, the Paramount Theatre, and a parking lot. At the northwest corner of the Old Public Burial Ground, the Golden Ball garage opened in 1932. St. Malachy's Hall was demolished, replaced by the high school. The church at the corner of King Street East and Carmarthen, later the YWCA, is now an apartment building. At the top left was the Red Ball Brewery, Ganong's, and a gas station; they have been replaced by the SMT building and the Prince Edward Square mall. (Grew Coll., PIRP #2732.)

King's Square was laid out in 1844 using plans by H. W. Pitts and E. G. Vernon. By 1845 it was our "forest garden." In 1874, when this photograph was taken, the Square was described as "a beautiful plot of land . . . covered with large shade trees, most of which were planted at the time of the visit of the Prince of Wales to the city in 1860. In the centre of the Square . . . surrounded by an iron railing is a Fountain. . . ." (PIRP #2753.)

The Young Monument in King's Square, built in 1891, is shown here c. 1941. The plaque reads: "Erected as a Public Memorial to John Frederick Young, who in the nineteenth year of his age lost his life on the thirtieth day of October, A.D. 1890 in Courtenay Bay, Saint John, New Brunswick while endeavouring to rescue Frederick E. Mundee from drowning. Greater love hath no man than this, that a man lay down his life for his friend." (Spinney Coll., PIRP #5927.)

The Common Council appointed a committee to select a location for a burial ground in 1786. A second committee was appointed in 1788. It was not until 1790 before mention was made that a burial ground had in fact been selected and was then in use. The following year the Council passed its bylaw regulating the use of the said ground. The graveyard closed in 1848. This view of the main path, c. 1880, shows a fence in the background, wood benches, and several maintenance workers. (Courtesy PANB.)

"The old Burying Ground is the only public place in the city, where citizens and strangers can enjoy themselves in beholding the loveliness of flowers in all their beauty of foliage, blooms, and fragrance . . ." It is shown here c. 1890. (Courtesy NAC.)

"Children use the old graveyard as a playground, and gleefully dance around and upon the fallen stones . . . It was left to a man working about the premises today to do the final act of desecration. The axe which he was using became dull, and he calmly and deliberately walked over to one of the weather beaten headstones, and on it sharpened the blade of the axe . . . It is in this manner that the memory of the Loyalists is kept." This is a c. 1928 photograph. (Courtesy NBM.)

In 1959 Thomas Cummins' wood tablet marker was in the southwest corner of the plot which now holds the Irving Christmas tree. (Courtesy NBM.)

Seven
Militia Artillery

The 3rd N.B. Regiment, Canadian Artillery, was formed in Saint John on May 4, 1793. This is the oldest artillery unit in the country. To commemorate its centennial, Captain J. B. M. Baxter wrote the first one-hundred-year history of the regiment. The unit formed outside the drill shed at the Barrack Green for this 1896 photograph. Standing on the boardwalk to the rear of the band is Sergeant Major Hughes. The commanding officer, Lieutenant Colonel John R. Armstrong, is in front of the unit. Captain J. B. M. Baxter is the ninth from the left in the front row. Baxter commanded the regiment from 1907 to 1912. (3RCA Coll., PIRP #3162.)

Former Mayor and Lieutenant Governor D. L. MacLaren served with the artillery on Partridge Island and overseas during World War I. He was wounded in France and had a leg amputated. After the war he had this dugout reconstructed in the basement of his home on Coburg Street. He and his wartime colleagues would meet here on Saturday evenings to play cards, have a few drinks, and tell old war stories. (Graham Coll., PIRP #4938.)

Summer training camp for the militia usually meant a trip to Petewawa, Ontario, the artillery training area. These gunners are the signallers of the 3rd Medium Brigade in 1934. The duty of a signaller was to relay information, either by flag or lamp, from the observation officer back to the gun position. For some, this annual training was an important source of income during the lean years of the Depression. Buzz Devenne (back row, fourth from the left), joined the regiment in 1926 and served until 1962. Buzz won several prizes in his early years for his signalling skills. (Devenne Coll., PIRP #4886.)

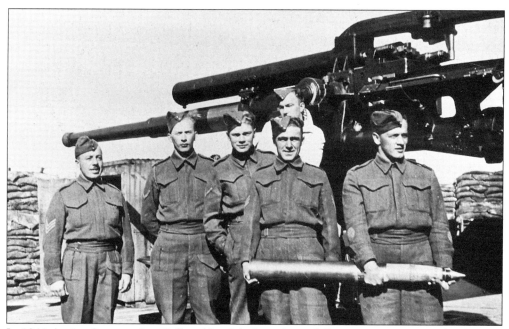

In 1941 Acting Sergeant Les Cull and his 8th Anti-Aircraft Battery gun crew posed in front of the 3.7-inch gun at Fort Howe. The first four men, from the left to right, are: Les Cull, Bombadier R. Collins, Bombadier Clifton Lovett, and Sergeant Ollie Cormier. The other two men have not yet been identified. (Devenne Coll., PIRP #1164.)

Gunner Bill Hull served with the 15th Coast Battery on Partridge Island from 1941 to 1945. He spent two years working in the Battery Observation Post (shown here in 1942). From here the location of a vessel approaching the harbour would be plotted and the information transmitted to the guns and to the fire command centre at the Martello Tower. Bill is relaying data to the guns in case "an action" is required. (Hull Coll., PIRP #3085.)

On October 23, 1955, Major James H. Turnbull, the commanding officer of the 104th MAA Battery, paraded his battery to the Church of the Good Shephard on Manawagonish Road. His Honour Lieutenant Governor and Mrs. D.L. MacLaren attended the service, and later took the salute at the march past on Main Street, Lancaster. After the parade the officers and men went to the unit headquarters on Courtenay Hill. (McGoldrick Coll., PIRP #5129.)

The 3rd (N.B.) Medium Anti-Aircraft Regiment (MAA) went to Picton, Ontario, to conduct anti-aircraft training. In 1957 the regiment was awarded the Turnbull Trophy for efficiency in "ack-ack" training, the last unit to win this trophy. (Schofield Coll., PIRP #5554.)

The senior NCO's of the 3rd Field Artillery Regiment (The Loyal Company) posed outside the Armoury for this informal group shot in July 1966. WO2 Tom Keleher (second from right), RSM Pat Donovan (third from right), and his son, Sgt. Ron Donovan (fourth from right) have been positively identified; Al Christie, Cecil Maxwell, Fergie Price, and Bob Clayton are also in the photograph. (Donovan Coll., PIRP #6161.)

Lieutenant Colonel Reg Sansom (right) turned over command of the 3rd Field Artillery Regiment (The Loyal Company) to Lieutenant Colonel James H. Turnbull (centre) in February 1965. Brigadier Philip W. Oland, the Honourary Colonel, is at the left. (3RCA Coll., PIRP #3131.)

In May 1974 the Royal Canadian Artillery Association (The Loyal Company) dedicated this 6-inch howitzer to their fallen comrades in a ceremony at Fort Howe. From left to right are: Father David Bona, Brigadier Philip W. Oland, and Gunners Pat Donovan, Olive Fournier, Leo Mulholland, Bob Lockhart, Clarence Steele, Elmer Diblee, Hilton Dixon, Clarey Mason, and Bill Schofield. (PIRP #4065.)

Eight
Marching Bands

The City Cornet Band, formed in 1874, built the bandstand in King's Square. Their first concert there was on August 8, 1908. An original member of the band, James Connolly, is at the left with the euphonium. Robert McCarthy, treasurer, is at the right with the E Bass. Other members at the concert were: Dan Gallagher, John McMahon, H. McQuade, P. McMahon, P.M. Higgins, John Bardsley, W.F. Hanneberry, John Butler, M.J. Higgins, Robert Clarke, Warren Terry, Fred Hazel, James Robinson, Fred Elliott, Joe Hazel, Vince Kelly, L. McNamara, H. McMahon, H. Bridgeo, W.D. Connolly, D. Higgins, James Myers, J. Kinsella, W. O'Connor, and Leo McCarthy. (Connolly Coll., PIRP #237.)

The Bishop held annual Sunday school picnics at Torryburn. The picnic was described as the "official charity of the parish as the proceeds go towards the support of the orphans in St. Vincent's Convent and the Boy's Industrial Home at Silver Falls." The City Cornet Band led the procession from the St. Malachy's and St. Joseph's Schools to the train station at Mill Street. The first train usually left at 10 am, with the last train returning at 8 pm. The band gave concerts all day, while the children enjoyed games and refreshments. In this c. 1938 photograph, Walter Donnelly is the third band member from the right, and Billy Bridgeo, playing the flute, is behind him. (Donnelly Coll., PIRP #275.)

The Carleton Cornet Band of West Saint John was formed in 1891. In 1920 they temporarily changed their name to the Martello Cornet Band. In this c. 1940 photograph on Union Street, three members have been identified: Bill Lanyon (the bandmaster) Ralph Akerley (front row, third from right) and Alan Craig (second row, fourth from left). (Akerley Coll., PIRP #5069.)

For many years, HMCS *Brunswicker* either had its own pipe and drum band or used the services of the Caledonia pipe band. This early 1950s view shows their brass and reed band on Main Street, Lancaster. The bandmaster at the rear of the band is Philip Sydney Brodie. In the background can be seen familiar Lancaster landmarks: Horslers Drug Store, the Gaiety Theatre, Horslers Gift Shop, and the Fountain Restaurant. (James Coll., PIRP #4447.)

Captain Bruce Holder Sr., bandmaster of the 3rd (NB) Medium Anti-Aircraft Regiment, RCA, leads his band down Main Street west in 1955. The band was leading the 104th MAA Battery from its annual church parade. In 1947 Captain Holder was appointed master of the reconstituted band, and made it one of the finest military bands in Eastern Canada in the 1950s and 1960s. He was succeeded in command of the band by his son Bruce Jr. (McGoldrick Coll., PIRP #5130.)

Nine
Harbour

For over one hundred years, residents made the ferry trip across the harbour. Navy Island is clearly visible behind the ferry *Ludlow*, c. 1910. The channel between the island and the west side was called Buttermilk Channel. Both the island and channel disappeared with port expansion in the early 1930s. The sign on the building in the foreground reads "Horses Not Allowed." (PIRP #430.)

On August 21, 1894, the yacht *Primrose*, in the Corporation Cup race, was struck by a squall off Mahogany Island and sank. Eight men drowned: Samuel Hutton (a member of the Paris crew), Fred Priest, George Heathfield, Albert Akerly, Henry Bartlett, James Hurley, William Russell, and Harry Hoyt. The four survivors were: Howard Holder, Thomas H. Miles, Fred S. Heans, and James McKeever. On August 28, with just her mast and sails visible, the *Primrose* was raised and towed to Sand Point. Only the body of Harry Hoyt was recovered. (Herrington Coll., PIRP #4386.)

In the 1870s Market Square was still the commercial centre for the uptown. Thomas H. Reed's Peoples House (drug store) was at the foot of Dock Street. Robinson Brothers was at the foot of King Street (on the right). The wagons and slovens in the Square were available for hire. On June 20, 1877, all of this was destroyed by fire. (Courtesy PANB.)

The tug *Holly* is seen in one of the slips at the west side. The scows at the left were used for anything from coal refuelling to loading cargo. The camouflaged ship on the right is a reminder that in 1917, Saint John was a major port for the shipment of war supplies overseas. (Fowler Coll., PIRP #6510.)

This 1918 image shows Protection Street in the foreground, with Reeds Point and the Lower Cove across the harbour. The arrival of the CPR in 1889 meant that the homes on Protection Street would have to share their neighbourhood not only with grain elevators, but also with tracks and boxcars. Across the harbour at the left can be seen two camouflaged ships, another reminder of wartime. (Fowler Coll., PIRP #6527.)

The schooner *Katherine V. Mills* at North Market Slip, c. 1920, may have brought goods for the Barbour Company, or C.T. Merritt, marine and stationary engines, or the Imperial Tobacco Company at 15 Mill Street. The chimney of the Dock Street Power Plant can be seen in the background. (PIRP #436.)

On April 23, 1928, the ferry *Ludlow* crashed into the southern wing of the east side ferry entrance. The report on the accident, written by Fred S. Heans, master carpenter (who survived the sinking of the *Primrose* in 1894) and Captain A. J. Mulchay, port warden, found the accident to have been caused by the freshet "swinging the vessel out of position." Seventy-two feet of piling and sheathing fell across the *Ludlow*, doing damage to its upper structure. The passengers were standing at the other end of the ferry preparing to disembark. Some $20,000 in damage was done to the ferry, the pier, and the tug *Neptune*. (Belyea Coll., PIRP #4624.)

The harbour on December 21, 1928, had at least thirteen vessels in port. In the foreground can be seen the mill pond with the lumber scows of Mackay lumber, and the rail trestle behind Acadia Street. Fort Howe has always been the best vantage point to watch harbour operations. (PIRP #461.)

The schooner *Avon Queen*, registered in Bridgetown, Barbados, is at North Market Slip, *c.* 1933. The *Avon Queen* was built in Hantsport, N.S., as the *Jessie Louise Farquier*. She was lost on a voyage from Turks Island with salt for Saint John in 1937. There are several smaller fishing vessels at the south slip. Market Slip, the celebrated landing spot of the Loyalists, was partially filled in for a parking lot in the 1960s. (PIRP #4395.)

The staff of the Customs Department at the west side is shown here on April 21, 1930. The following members have been identified: (front row) Packy MacFarlane (far left) and ? Logan (fourth from left); (middle row) Cecil Folkins (second from left), George H. Hayter (third from left), Edward Puddy (fourth from left), William T. "Pappy" Lanyon (fifth from left, the bandmaster of the Carleton Cornet Band), and George Hazelwood (seventh from left); (back row) Cecil Herrington (second from left) and Curtis Willis (fourth from left, with glasses). (Herrington Coll., PIRP #5081.)

The *Saint John* arrived here on May 3, 1932. She carried passengers between Saint John, Digby, and Boston. The overnight service to Boston cost $10 one way. The *Saint John* offered dancing under the "rainbow-hued dome of the Terrace Ball Room panelled in silver and ebony" and meals in a great blue and gold dining hall, in addition to an Elizabethan smoking room, a library, a music room, and comfortable staterooms. (Wills Coll, PIRP #776.)

On November 24, 1944, the CPSS *Beaverhill* went aground on Hilyards Reef, carrying 3,846 bags of overseas mail and 2,300 cases of ammunition. The mail was recovered, and in June 1945, Dean Hatfield of St. Martins received the contract to dump the ammunition in 100 fathoms of water. Instead, he took most of it to St. Martins, where local residents removed the brass and sold some 17 tons of it to J.J. Freedman at South Market Slip. The RCMP may never have found out about the operation had it not been for an explosion and fire at the St. Martins wharf in mid-August 1945. On March 22, 1946, the last boxes of ammunition were taken off the *Beaverhill*. In December 1946, the stern of the vessel was towed to sea and sunk. The bow was not disposed of until early 1947. (Rourke Coll., PIRP #3011.)

On July 31, 1954, the ferry *Loyalist* was towed from the city enroute to Chatham. Built in Shelburne, N.S., in 1933, she carried thousands of area residents on daily trips until Common Council decided in October 1951 to remove the ferry from service. Extensions kept her in the city until 1954. With the departure of the *Loyalist*, a service which began with the *Victoria* in 1839 ended. (PIRP #446.)

The Market Slip fishing fleet, c. 1953, was soon to become a thing of the past. Pollution, overfishing, and physical changes to the Slip saw a decline in the number of residents and neighbours fishing the harbour and bay. In August 1959, when the bottom photograph was taken, the harbour salmon industry was still a viable operation. Bill Bartlett (left) and James Wilson (right) are passing #10 shed on the west side in their salmon skiff. Today, a few fishing sheds on Riverview Drive are the only visible reminders of Saint John's once viable harbour fishing industry. (PIRP #157–20; Bartlett Coll., PIRP #5198.)

The city government owned and leased harbour facilities until 1927, when title was sold to the federal government. In 1929 the port facilities included fifteen ocean berths (ten with grain conveyors), three grain elevators, two rail lines (CN and CP), a fertilizer storage shed, three frost-free potato warehouses, coal and oil bunkering facilities, molasses tanks, an immigration depot with hospitals at Partridge Island, a Seamen's Institute, and a good towing system and stevedores that were "highly efficient." (Courtesy SJPC.)

Grain has been a major export through the port since the end of the nineteenth century. The CPR owned two elevators on the west side, and the CNR one at the foot of Water Street. The total capacity in 1929 was 2,225,000 bushels. By 1947 the capacity had expanded to 3,500,000 bushels. The longshoremen are filling bags bound for Port Sudan, a gift of the World Food Program. All three grain elevators have since been demolished. Both this photograph and the one at the top of the page were taken c. 1972. (Courtesy SJPC.)

Ten
Partridge Island

James Wilson and his family lived here from 1857 until 1900. James (right) was the lightkeeper, bell-alarm keeper, signal master, gas maker, and first engineer of Robert Foulis' steam fog-whistle. He is shown here c. 1880. (Courtesy NBM.)

A new 80-candlepower condensed light with a 45-mile range was installed in 1915. (Ennis Coll., PIRP #5994.)

Fred Hargrove's residence is shown here c. 1910. Fred was a quarantine stewart, and lived on the island until 1927. His brother, Jim, was also a stewart until 1942. (Hargrove Coll., PIRP #1958.)

During World War I over two thousand troops trained on the island. These gunners were the first contingent from the 3rd Canadian Garrison Artillery to leave Partridge Island for Valcartier, August 29, 1914, enroute to France. (Courtesy NBM.)

Georgie and Henry Bisson lived on the island from 1926 until 1932. Their father, George Bisson, was a quarantine stewart. When Henry enlisted for World War II service, he was sent to the island for garrison duty. (Bisson Coll., PIRP #230.)

Henry Bisson's report card of June 1930. He was first in his class of two students. (Bisson Coll., PIRP #231.)

Jean McCallum taught on the island for eight years, ending in 1933. On this day, May 23, 1930, she received two apples. Many remember Jean through her work with the radio and newspaper in the 1950s and 1960s as Jean Sweet. (Hargrove Coll., PIRP #1959.)

The Celtic cross was erected in 1927 in memory of the Irish who died in 1847. Memorial services, like this one in September 1936, continued until World War II. They have recently been re-instituted. (Legere Coll., PIRP #4960.)

Partridge Island, photographed on April 3, 1941. (Coast Guard Coll., PIRP #2690.)

Eleven
Celebrations

Macaulay Bros. & Co., at 61–63 King Street, celebrated the September 1885 opening of the cantilever rail bridge at the Reversible Falls with this parade float. The bridge, built for the St. John Railway Bridge & Extension Company, was constructed by the Montreal Bridge Company. The CPR replaced this bridge with the current bridge in 1923. The businesses shown in the background are: Scovil, Fraser & Co. and O'Brien's bookstore at Vernon's Corner; William Gibson, watchmaker; Mank & Co., furrier; and Louis Green, tobacconist. (PIRP #562.)

For many decades the city's labour organizations held Labour Day parades in September. This c. 1908 parade on Brussells Street (later renamed Prince Edward) shows the Longshoremen's Association turning onto Union Street. The banner is the same one carried in 1853 to mark construction of the European & North American Railway to Shediac. Further back, the men are pulling a model of the ship *Robert Reed*. The New Brunswick Museum has this ship model and the banner. (PIRP #3591.)

The Mill Street arch (corner of Smythe Street) was one of four built for the visit of the Duke and Duchess of Cornwall and York on October 17, 1901. During the visit, the Duke and Duchess presented medals to South African War veterans and new colours to the 62nd Saint John Fusiliers. The arches were only temporary, and were demolished after the departure of the royal visitors. (Dicks Coll., PIRP #2383.)

The tercentenary of the arrival of DeMonts and Champlain on June 24, 1604, was marked by a a crowded gathering of over twenty thousand people at Market Square. Historical accuracy was not part of the program. The natives were portrayed by members of the Neptune Rowing Club, and activities included a re-enactment of an attack against DeMonts' vessel from Navy Island. His vessel, *L'Acadie*, was not a replica but actually a barge with a fake bow and stern. Such details were of no consequence to the assembled multitude. The crews from visiting warships, over one thousand militia, five bands, firemen, and many others, gathered at Market Square to hear the Lieutenant Governor, Premier and Mayor White read proclamations and give speeches. The parade then proceeded to Riverview Memorial Park on Douglas Avenue, where the South African War memorial was dedicated. In the public library a plaque to DeMonts and Champlain was unveiled (the plaque can now be seen at the library in Market Square). That evening the firemen had a parade and there was an "illuminated marine pageant on the harbor." (Fawcett Coll., PIRP #577.)

The "John Bull and his Allies" prize-winning float in the Joy Day parade on August 14, 1919. Preceding the float were: Lieutenant Logan, S.M. Raynor, Corporal Chapman, Gunner Harry Sibley, and Private F.T. Wood. On the float were: Edward Harding, James W. Cook, George Leaver, James Mills, S.M. Tremain, Willa Carloss, Bernice Smith, Arthur S. Lewis, H. Smith, and C.H. Nixon. Sapper Walter Brindle is at the right. (Willis Coll., PIRP #785.)

HRH The Prince of Wales is flanked on his left by Lieutenant Governor William Pugsley and on his right by His Excellency the Governor General, the Duke of Devonshire. The Prince landed at Reeds Point on August 15, 1919. Despite the rain, he visited with patients at the Lancaster Military Hospital at Jewett's Castle and presented colours to the 26th N.B. Battalion. (PIRP #6538.)

On July 10, 1932, the police and the Carleton Cornet Band led the Loyal Orange Lodge down Mill Street. The parade, at the corner of Paradise Row, reveals much about city streets at this time. The streets were covered with paving block (not cobblestones), and a double set of streetcar tracks ran along Mill up to Main. Just before Smythe Street are the road gates of the CNR. (Harned Coll., PIRP #3585.)

On June 1, 1935, over three thousand scouts and guides assembled at the Barrack Green to see the Chief Scout and Guide, Lord and Lady Baden Powell. At 3 pm that day the Chief Scout and Guide drove on to the Exhibition Grounds, where the grandstand was full of enthusiastic parents. The scouts and guides "hurled into every activity—rope spinning, friction fire, bridge building, first aid, tent pitching, jungle dancers." The visit of Lord and Lady Baden Powell coincided with the Provincial Jamboree which formed part of the King's Jubilee Celebrations and Transportation Festival. (PIRP #4291.)

"Boy O boy, didja see the lines 'n' taggers 'n' elefuns didja?" That phrase must have been spoken hundreds of times on June 27, 1938, when the Robbins Brothers Circus performed at the East End ball field. There were over two hundred performers, and several of the artists also gave performances at the orphanages and the children's hospitals. After the show some lucky ones got behind the Big Top for a picture. From left to right above: Happy Kellems, Gordie Crockett, an unidentified clown, Charlie Lynch, and Van Wells. From left to right below: Mrs. Gordie Crockett, an unidentified young woman, "the stellar attraction Hoot Gibson, famous Western movie star and the champion cowboy of the world," another unidentified young woman, and Virginia Lynch. (Lynch Coll., PIRP #6810 and 6812.)

On June 13, 1939, tens of thousands of citizens and visitors crammed the streets trying to catch a glimpse of their king and queen. This was the first visit to Canada of a reigning monarch, and King George VI and Queen Elizabeth proved to be popular. They arrived at the Fairville train station and then toured the city by motorcade, shown here at the foot of King at Prince William Street. At the end of their visit they returned to the Union Station where thousands gathered to see them off. Even fifty-five years after the event, people recall in detail where they were standing to see "their King and Queen." (Richards Coll., PIRP #5701 and #5704.)

Word of the end of the war in Europe unleashed emotions held in for over five years. Soon husbands, wives, sons, daughters, and friends, would be coming home. VE Day was celebrated at King's Square on May 8, 1945. A huge parade of veterans, soldiers, and schoolchildren made its way to the Square where the Mayor read the civic proclamation of peace and prayers of thanksgiving were offered. (Donovan Coll., PIRP #1044.)

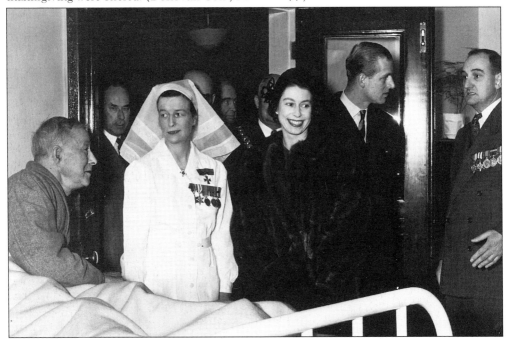

Her Royal Highness Princess Elizabeth and Prince Philip visited the Lancaster DVA Hospital on November 6, 1951. In 1939 tour officials inadvertently omitted this hospital from the visit of her parents, much to the chagrin of the patients. Her Royal Highness, also a veteran, spoke with Private Albert Angel (World War I), with Nursing Sister Sarah Miles (World War II) at her left. Prince Philip, also a World War II veteran, spoke with Lancaster Mayor Burt Heustis (World War II). When she next came to Saint John in 1959, Her Royal Highness again visited the hospital. (Richards Coll., PIRP #5719.)

Mayor George Howard hosted HRH Princess Elizabeth and Prince Philip at a state dinner in the Georgian Ballroom of the Admiral Beatty Hotel on November 6, 1951. Inside the hotel, veterans from the Boer War to World War II formed an honour guard. Mayor Howard presented the Princess with a thirty-one piece after-dinner coffee set on behalf of the citizens. (Graham Coll., PIRP #4930.)

Lieutenant Governor D.L. MacLaren read the proclamation incorporating the City of Lancaster on January 1, 1953. Composed of the smaller communities of Milford, Fairville, Randolf, and Barnhill, Lancaster was a city whose days were numbered. In 1967 Saint John swallowed up Lancaster in an amalgamation that many likened to a "shotgun wedding." (MacPherson Coll., PIRP #6024.)

On May 12, 1953, city employees Earle Biddiscombe, Richard Walsh, Jack Spinney, Herb Fawcett, and A.V.F. Duffy put the finishing touches to a number of signs which went up for the week-long coronation celebrations of Her Majesty Elizabeth II, Queen of Canada. The celebrations included street dances, a parade of Shriners, Cubs, Scouts, Brownies, and Guides, a go-cart race, a decorated doll-carriage parade, and a track and field event. (Spinney Coll., PIRP #5920.)

Pipe Major Lofty McMillan was a towering figure in many parades of the 1950s and 1960s. Shown here leading the Caledonia Pipe Band down Waterloo Street, c. 1955, many remember Lofty also for his years as a police officer, a labour leader, and a member of Common Council. The Canadian Tire store is now Albert's Draperies. (PIRP #157–30.)

Twelve
Shipbuilding

On June 11, 1918, at 2 pm, thousands crowded the shores near the Reversible Falls to witness the launching of the four-masted schooner *Dornfontein*. Built by D.A. Saker of the Marine Construction Company Canada Ltd., she was laid down in October 1917. She was 172 feet in length, had a beam of 40 feet, and a registered tonnage of 695 tons. The keel was made of Douglas fir, with other woods such as birch, Bay Shore spruce, and Virginia oak also used in her construction. The *Dornfontein* left the city fully loaded and carrying a large deck load of lumber on July 31 for Natal, South Africa. She was 25 miles off Brier Island (Nova Scotia) when a German submarine surfaced and fired two shots across her bow. "After taking from the ship all her valuables and foodstuffs, as well as a large quantity of gasoline . . . the Germans started a fire in her forecastle and another in her aftercabin, and the ship burned to the water's edge." (Jones Coll., PIRP #5900.)

The 2,300-ton wooden steamer *War Moncton* was launched from the Grant & Horne shipyard at Courtenay Bay on May 29, 1919. During the launch, the *War Moncton*'s anchors were supposed to check her as she left the ways, but instead her stern stuck fast in the mud. It took ten minutes for the tugs *Neptune*, *Alice R.*, and *G.D. Hunter* to move her. She was then towed to pier no. 6 to receive her engines. The *War Moncton* and her sister ship, the *War Fundy*, were built for the Imperial Munitions Board. As the war had ended, the *War Moncton* did not see active service and was scrapped not long after her completion. (PIRP #6155; Reid Coll, PIRP #4516.)

In May 1930, Fred Lord of Navy Island caulked the motorboat *Milwaulkee*. Fred and his brother Charles made annual trips up the St. John River to Grand Lake for eels, which they exported to the United States. Fred was killed in November 1930, in an accident at the port. Navy Island had originally been reserved for the Royal Navy but the City leased the land to fishermen. In 1927 the City sold Navy Island to the federal government. (French Coll., PIRP #3120.)

The Saint John Dry Dock and Shipbuilding Company, Limited, billed itself as one of the largest in the world. The outer dock, with the CPSS *Marloch*, was 650 feet long, and the inner dock, with the SS *Emperor of Montreal* and the dredge *Leaconfield*, was 500 feet long. When this photograph was taken, *c.* 1930, the yard had a marine railway dock system, electrically-operated pumps, ten 15-ton electric capstans, one 15-ton travelling crane, and one 60-ton fixed derrick on the fitting-out wharf. (PIRP #821.)

This 1947 view of the drydock shows just how busy the yard was. There are ten large vessels tied up at the yard, with another eight smaller vessels, from tugs to barges, nearby. There are also vessels tied up at the fertilizer plant pier and the Irving Oil tank farm. Near the top right of the photograph is the old Poor House on Bayside Drive. Across the street was the entrance to the Boys Industrial Home. (Phinney Coll., PIRP #467.)

Thirteen
Transportation

This may be the first car in Saint John, *c.* 1904. While the owners and the type of car are not identified, the background gives us a clue as to where they were. J. Johnston was a house and sign painter at 101–103 Princess Street. William Crawford repaired and sold sewing machines next door at 105 1/2. (James Coll., PIRP #6152.)

Although there were plans for an airport here as early as 1920, this unidentified airplane made use of the Courtenay Bay mud flats for its landing, c. 1910. The number of onlookers indicate that an airplane was very much an oddity. Our airport at Millidgeville opened in 1929. (Lt. Col. GGK Holder Coll., PIRP #5556.)

On June 29, 1911, McAvity & Sons Ltd. registered this Reo, shown here outside their store on King Street. In 1911 a new motor vehicle act was passed by the N.B. Legislature. It doubled to ten the number of days before you had to register your vehicle after purchase; it provided for two license plates; the speed limit in "built-up" areas was increased to 15 mph; and it made tail lamps mandatory. There were 216 vehicles registered to Saint John owners between 1905 and 1912, when this photograph was taken. Automobiles were still a sufficient curiosity to attract the attention of the two children and young boy on the sidewalk. (O'Leary Coll, PIRP #369.)

The Saint John Railway Co. staff posed for a photograph outside the Wentworth Street car barn on August 14, 1919. The Beacon light float was in the Soldiers Joy Day parade (several of the men in the front left are still in military uniform). Car #71, with its destination board reading "Seaside Park," appears inside the barn just above the horse; an ex-Buffalo car (left), an 80-class car (centre), and a Tillsonburg car (left) are also present. (Thomas Coll., PIRP #4259.)

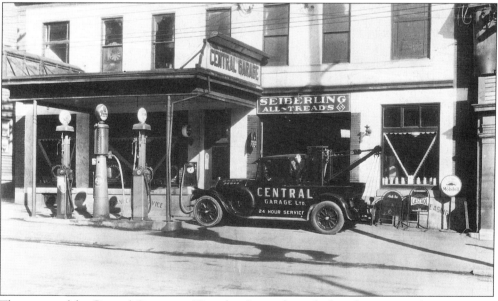

The owner of the Central Garage on Waterloo Street showed a bit of ingenuity when it came to getting a tow truck. The vehicle is a 1928 Pearce Arrow sedan with the rear half of the car cut out, and a tow crane installed. The garage sold Imperial Premium gas, Castrol and Mobil motor oil, and Seiberling tires. The building still stands as the Waterloo medical clinic. (Richards Coll., PIRP #5678.)

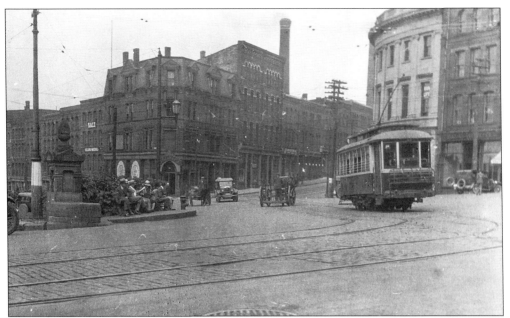

For two weeks in late August 1929, Lawrence Young of Montreal, an amateur photographer, and his wife spent their vacation in the city. His photograph album records many city scenes of that period. At Market Square he captured four modes of transportation: a wagon, a car, a sloven, and a streetcar. From 1869 to 1948 horses, wagons, and pedestrians shared the roadway with streetcars. (Young Coll., PIRP #3207.)

On June 14, 1939, CNR locomotive #6028 took the Royal Train, with Their Majesties King George VI and Queen Elizabeth aboard, from the Union Station to Sackville. The previous day they arrived at the Fairville Station by train, and then proceeded by motorcade through the city, until they arrived at the Union Station. Preparing the train for its journey are Don Kirkpatrick (fourth from left) and Richard Smith (second from right). (Thomas Coll., PIRP #5551.)

Ferries have been used to cross both the St. John and Kennebecasis Rivers for over 150 years. This is the Gondola Point ferry crossing the Kennebecasis, c. 1940. (Hastings Coll., PIRP #4319.)

George S. deForest & Sons, wholesale grocers, used this 1948 GMC as their delivery truck. The driver at the left, Bert Day, drove for deForest for another two years before he joined Canadian National Railway, where he worked as a motorman for thirty-five years. The driver of the 1947 Ford is unidentified. George S. deForest & Sons had been at North Market wharf since the 1880s. (B. Day Coll., PIRP #6975.)

Ellis Motors Ltd. on Rothesay Avenue offered a new car showroom as well as a crane wrecker service and repair shop. The new car showroom pictured features 1949 Ford Monarchs. The ambulance is an International panel truck, and to the right of the telephone pole is a 1948 Ford 1/2-ton pickup. In June 1952, Wilson's Sales & Service moved from Waterloo Street to here, and on December 11, 1952, reopened as Wilson's Motors. Brett Motors occupies the building today. (Edwards Coll., PIRP #4148.)

The new 1962 Ford Galaxie V8 had just been unveiled at Downey Ford on Crown Street when this photograph was taken. Downey's has been in business since 1951, and moved to Crown Street in 1959. (PIRP #7149.)

Fourteen
Schools and Churches

The St. Thomas School on Erin Street opened in 1910. Situated at the corner of Brunswick Street, thousands of Irish and Lebanese children from the East End were taught here. The school was demolished under the urban renewal scheme of the 1950s and 1960s. (Legere Coll., PIRP #6137.)

Eugenia Kelly's first grade class had perfect attendance the day this photograph was taken in the Fairville Superior School on Easter, 1938. The students are, from front to back, from left to right row: (first row) Alberta Craft, Kenneth Olsen, Eloise Allen, Ora Belling, Robert Campbell, and Norman Duff; (second row) Alice Horncastle, Sammy Koven, Alastair MacPherson, Frances Gabel, and Grace Craft; (third row) Stanley Magee, Murray Keirstead, Vaughan Worden, Shirley Galbraith, Jack Magee, and Leslie Stymest; (fifth row) Harry Comeau, Vivien Burns, Joan Losier, Jock Armstrong, Norman Hicks, and Lillian Macdonald; (sixth row) Murray Stevens, Gordon Jenkins, Elva Patterson, Walter Jones, Robert Damery, and Ann Waddell; (seventh row) Evelyn Hamilton, Rhoda Nelson, and Arvilla Craft. (Magee Coll., PIRP #4500.)

The history of St. Vincent's Boys and Girls Schools predate this century. In the 1920s the City Cornet Band held theatrical performances to raise money for the school. By the time this photograph was taken in 1950, the days of it being an all-boys school were coming to a close. In the mid-1950s St. Malachy's School opened as an all-boys school, with St. Vincent's reverting to all-girls status. (PIRP #704.)

The Boys' Industrial Home opened in 1893 in the former Saint John Penitentiary on Bayside Drive. The object of the home was the "training and reformation of delinquent boys under the age of sixteen." In addition to farm training, the boys also received industrial training and religious instruction, and participated in the scouting and cadet programs. As some boys had little formal education, a school program was instituted. In October 1951 the teacher accepted a portrait of the King and Queen, probably from the IODE. (PIRP #5789.)

Dufferin and St. Peter's Boys' Schools on Elm Street are shown in this c. 1973 photograph. In addition to their role as a place to educate youth, these schools also fulfilled various community functions. The Irish plays at St. Peter's, from the 1920s to the 1960s, are well-known. In 1920 the Girls' Glee Club of North End schools put on a programme of music, featuring Morley McLaughlin's *My Own Canadian Home*, as well as *My Own Kentucky Home*, *The Harp that once through Tera's Hall*, and *Rule Britannia*. Dufferin School was demolished in the mid-1970s; St. Peters was demolished in 1995. (G. McLaughlin Coll., PIRP #6940.)

The Lower Cove Church on Main Street (renamed Broad after the 1877 fire), was the Imperial Garrison Church until the departure of British troops after Confederation. Standing outside the church in 1863 is Major Morris' Royal Artillery choir. This building was destroyed in the Great 1877 Fire and was replaced by the current St. James Church. (Major J.M. Grant Coll., PIRP #2187.)

The cornerstone for the Queen Square Methodist Church was laid in August 1879. The church was described as "another handsome Gothic structure of red freestone and trim." It seated 750 people and another 250 when the Sunday school was added. A declining congregation saw amalgamation with Centenary Church in 1939. The building was eventually sold to the Salvation Army, who used it as a hostel during World War II. The Salvation Army demolished the church in June 1951. (PIRP #1866.)

The cornerstone of the Cathedral of the Immaculate Conception was laid on April 25, 1853, with the first mass being held on Christmas Eve, 1855. For the centennial of its consecration, Bishop Gilbert wrote, "Those of us who hold the Cathedral dear to our hearts will gladly recognize that now it is our turn to build—not a new Church, but a renovated Cathedral which will withstand the effects of time . . . It is a worthy and important task which will ensure the continuing presence of the Cathedral as an inspiration to us all." (PIRP #4354.)

The Ludlow Street United Baptist Church was at the corner of Ludlow and Duke Streets. In 1924 the pastor was Reverend A. Robbins. His son Carl started Robbins Drug store on Charlotte Street. The church was later demolished and replaced by a Dominion store that is now used by Frenchy' clothing store. (Hoyt Coll., PIRP #3202.)

The Victoria Street United Baptist Church was built in 1920 on a design by H. Claire Mott. This congregation organized in 1878, and soon after built a meetinghouse, without tower, holding five hundred people. It became too small for the growing congregation and on July 20, 1920, Reverend Hudson turned the first sod at the corner of Victoria and Durham Streets. The church opened for regular service in 1921 but by 1972 the structure had deteriorated to a point where repairs were too costly. Instead of repairs the congregation joined with Main Street Baptist Church, and in December 1973 the Victoria Street church was demolished. (Edwards Coll., PIRP #4164.)

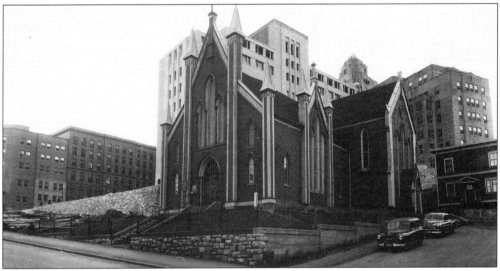

St. Mary's Anglican Church on Waterloo Street, the second "free church" of the Anglican Communion in Saint John, served its community from 1860 until 1967. From 1865 the General Public Hospital (which became the General Hospital in 1930) was its neighbour on Vinegar Hill. By the early 1960s the hospital dwarfed the church. Deconsecrated on September 27, 1967, the church was demolished for a planned hospital expansion which never happened. St. Mary's amalgamated with St. Bartholomew's on Westmorland Road in 1967. (PIRP #6692.)

Holy Trinity Church on Rockland Road, c. 1940, differed little from when the church first opened. The cornerstone was laid in 1890 and the first mass was celebrated by Reverend J. J. Walsh on July 2, 1892. In 1901 the interior decorations were completed, the stained-glass windows having been added in 1899–1900. Holy Trinity School opened in 1923 and the nearby Zion church was purchased and converted into a parish hall. The Zion church was demolished when the school needed to expand in the late 1950s. (Quinn Coll., PIRP #2550.)

Fifteen
Sports

The first game of hockey in the city was played in 1892 when "a game was gotten up between the bank clerks of the city and the old students of Lennoxville College. It was played in the Singer Rink..." The Saint John Bicycle & Athletic (B&A) Club organized the first four-team league in 1893. By 1895 the Saint John Hockey League had expanded to five teams with outside competition from Nova Scotian teams. The B&A Club were the Intermediate Hockey Champions in 1897–98. From left to right are: George A. Hilyard, K.R. Inches, Walter A. Harrison, F.A. Dunbrack, C.F.A. Gregory, M.F. Sheraton, goalie G. Johnston, captain F.G. Sancton, Harry Frink, R.O. Skinner, and mascot Lorenzo (in front). The B&A grounds were located in the area of Seaton Street and closed in 1899. (PIRP #4471.)

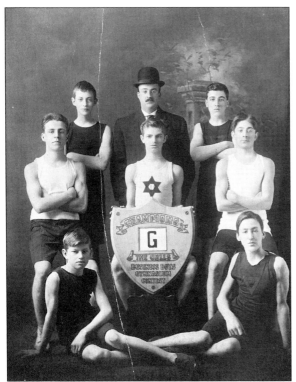

There were a few business colleges in operation in the early years of this century; Kerr's and Modern Business College were two of them. In 1911 the "Gulls" were the Business Boys Gym contest champions. From left to right are: (front row) Charles McKiel and Roy Roberts; (middle row) Harry W. Heans, captain Fred H. McKiel, and O.W. Leob; (back row) W.A. Thorne, physical director Edward F. Robertson, and Norman Robinson. (Searle Coll., PIRP #5983.)

Many people, like Alice E. Hoyt, took up the game of tennis. In May 1916 the nearest court to her home near Charles Street would have been beside Trinity Church. (O'Leary Coll., PIRP #344.)

Frank the "Boy Wonder" Logan followed in the skatesteps of his father Fred and brother Willie. His father was both the Canadian and International champion from 1907–1909, and Willie was New Brunswick's first Olympic medalist, winning two bronze medals in 1932. Although Frank did not reach the same international stature as his father and brother, he was still an outstanding speedskater. He won both the Canadian and International under 12 championships in 1925. He is shown here at Lily Lake, c. 1918. (PIRP #5007.)

Our speedskating champions were: Hugh McCormick, Hilton Belyea, Charlie Gorman, Fred, Willie, and Frank Logan, John Quigg, and Buddy Hamm. In 1951 Buddy captured the Canadian Juvenile Championship. Of the twenty competitions he raced between 1946 and 1951, Buddy (shown here) placed first nineteen times, and second once. He retired because "my interests started changing so I got out of it." (B. Hamm Coll., PIRP #6804.)

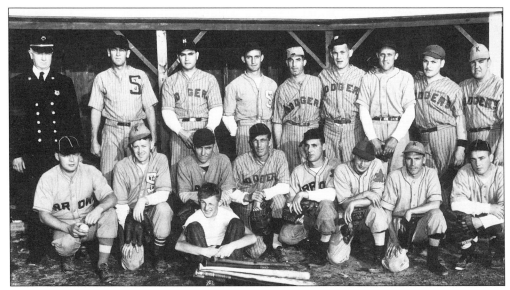

In 1943 Father Keough wanted a baseball team brought back to the North End, so he asked Oakie O'Connor of the South End Senior League to organize a team. In 1944 the St. Peter's squad captured the city title. Over the next fifteen or so years, games at St. Peter's attracted hundreds of spectators. The Saint John Fire Department team, shown here on August 24, 1950, consisted of Chief Holly Knight at the far left; others are Morris, Breen, Beyea, Secord, Jarvis, Coggins, Campbell, Raymond, Turner, Hayes, Joyce, Breen, Watters, Ramsey, Short, Godfrey, and Scott. (Spinney Coll., PIRP #5933.)

The 1957 War Amps Orioles were, from left to right: (front row) Albert Chenier, Wayne Keating, Dick Keating, Pat Hachey, Dan Doherty, Robert Chenier, coach A.L. Patterson, Brian Winchester, Tom McGratton, Larry Marr, Ron Dunham, and manager Hollis Case; (back row) captain Jim Keating, Al Nadeau, Gren Patterson, Terry Lockhart, and Brian Scott. (PIRP #3866.)

Sixteen
Public Buildings

The Asylum for the Insane was built in 1848 at Lancaster Heights, and was the first lunatic asylum in British North America. There have been several additions and name changes made to the building since this c. 1865 photograph was taken. Centracare will close in the fall of 1997. (PIRP #6044.)

The main Exhibition building on Sydney Street was built in 1880. The building was used for agricultural fairs, industrial expositions, and livestock shows. This annex was added in 1882. During World War I McAvity's used it for making 4.5-inch artillery ammunition. At the beginning of World War II it was used as a barracks. Both buildings were destroyed by fire in 1941. (McAvity Coll., PIRP #7159.)

The Imperial Theatre opened at Imperial Place in September 1913. *Grumpy* played there in 1920. In 1929 the theatre's name changed to Capitol. *Jivaro* and *Reap the Wild Wind* played there in the early 1950s. In 1957 it became the Full Gospel Assembly Church and in 1983 was purchased by the Bi-Capitol Project. The renovated theatre re-opened as a designated National Historic Site in 1994. (Golding Coll., PIRP #3055; James Coll., PIRP #3054.)

The Fairville Post Office on Main Street is shown here on July 1, 1927. This building is now Deluxe French Fries. (Hall Coll., PIRP #3599.)

The Knights of Pythias Good Cheer Council concert at the East Saint John Hospital was captured in this August 1927 photograph. (PIRP #3599.)

On July 28, 1924, Frank Ross, president of the Admiral Beatty Hotel Company, announced that construction of the Beatty would begin that same day on the site of the former Dufferin Hotel. The two-hundred-room, eight-storey, "absolutely fireproof" Beatty was our premier hotel from its opening in 1925. It closed in 1982. The Rotary Club, a construction partner in 1925, was once again a partner in its conversion to seniors' housing in 1985. This c. 1930 view shows the expansion at the rear of the Beatty as well as the garage further down Charlotte. (Titus Coll., PIRP #6842.)

The cornerstone for the New Brunswick Museum on Douglas Avenue was laid in June 1931. The museum opened on August 16, 1934, as part of New Brunswick's sesqui-centennial celebrations. Today, the building houses the Library and Archives Department, staff offices, and it is the Museum's storage warehouse. New exhibit facilities at Market Square were opened by HRH The Prince of Wales on April 28, 1996. (Edwards Coll., PIRP #4133.)

The Courthouse (built in 1829–30) and the fire station (built in 1840–41) are shown here in November 1947. The Courthouse, with its famous free-standing spiral staircase, suffered a disastrous fire in 1919. No. 2 fire hall is now the Fire Fighter's Museum. Both buildings are designated National Historic Sites. (Courtesy NAC.)

The Boys' Industrial Home on Bayside Drive, shown here in October 1951, opened in 1893 in the old Saint John Penitentiary. Intended to house forty-five boys, the complex at times housed as many as seventy-five. It closed on December 12, 1962. The property was transferred to the CNR but the building burned down on February 5, 1963. (PIRP #5787.)

The Custom House was designed by architects McKean & Fairweather and built between 1878 and 1880. The third storey of the pavilion contained an observatory for taking astronomical measurements, and the tower above contained a time ball for "giving the true time to nautical men." It was demolished in 1959–60. (PIRP #6694.)

The N.B. Protestant Orphanage on Manawagonish Road, shown here c. 1970, opened in 1924. This was followed with the construction of an infant's building in 1947. The orphanage closed in 1978. (PIRP #5630.)

Construction of the new city hall at Market Square began in 1969 and was completed in 1971. While in the seventh grade, the author and classmate John Miller were selected from their school to paint one of the panels on the fence around the construction site. (Kilcup Coll., PIRP #6853.)

Seventeen
Businesses

Market Square, c. 1865, reveals several things about how business was conducted and the types of goods available. G.M. Bayard and J.M. Walker offered drugs and medicines, dye wools and dye stuffs, paints, oils, and varnishes; Sheffield House included a pianoforte wareroom; Daniel & Boyd's London House offered clothing and dry goods; and W.O. Smith offered oils, varnishes, and medicines. A horse-drawn streetcar has just passed Chipman Hill, and there are slovens, carriages, and drays on the street. Note the gaslight fixture in front of Bayard & Walker. (Major JM Grant Coll., PIRP #2185.)

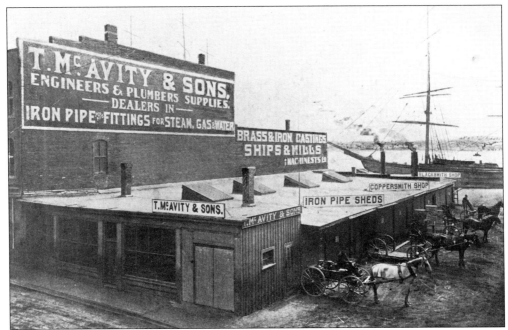

Thomas McAvity began his business on May 19, 1834. Initially a dry goods and wholesale hardware firm, the McAvity brass foundry was formed in 1863. Originally located on Princess and then Broad Street, the plant finally located on Water Street, where it is shown here, c. 1890. The signs leave little for the imagination as to what McAvity produced. The plant remained on Water Street until the 1950s. (PIRP #6051.)

The construction of the McAvity plant on Rothesay Avenue began on April 26, 1916. When there was a war going on, nothing was spared for an essential war industry—McAvity's opened for business on August 1, 1916. In 1918 the firm (renamed the Maritime Manufacturing Corporation and probably funded by the U.S. government) began to produce 9.2-inch ammunition for the American army. After the war the firm returned to making valves and other hardware, but it was the fire hydrant that made the company famous. McAvity hydrants are still made today by Clow Canada in the Grandview Avenue Industrial Park. The McAvity plant was demolished in 1985 and the Real Atlantic Superstore now occupies the site. (Lewis Coll., PIRP #4905.)

Hamm's grocery store at the corner of King and Ludlow Street west is shown here in February 1917. The calendar on the centre pole advertises "Smoke Master Mason—It's Good Tobacco." The sign hanging from the ceiling is for Dickeson's Tea, and the calender at the left is for Stag tobacco. Products on the shelves include: Catelli macaroni, Purity Oats, Cricso, Quaker Corn Meal, Surprise soap, Quaker Wheat, bread, Ogalvie Oats, and Hamm Brother's Cream Soda. From left to right are: James W. Hamm, Alva French, Charles P. Hamm, and Lillian Hamm. Charles later operated C.P. Hamm & Son's meat and groceries at 143 Charlotte Street, c. 1939. The signs advertise bananas at 19¢ a pound, sugar at 49¢ for 10 pounds with a $2 order, Robin Hood flour at 63¢ for a 24-pound bag, and spices at 8¢ a can. Around the corner, the Hamm family operated the Busy Bee Bakery, and they also operated grocery stores on King Street west, Rockland Road, and in Rothesay. (B. Hamm Coll., PIRP #6849; A. Hamm Coll., PIRP #7151.)

James W. Hamm operated his St. John Meat Co. at 213 Union Street in 1931–32. At Easter, vendors decorated their windows with the best Easter meats available. Citizens would go window shopping, trying to select the best display. The company name is inscribed in ice on the coolant bars just below the Swift's Premium Ham & Bacon oversized sign. Steak, chicken, various vegetables, eggs, Perfect Orange and Pineapple syrups, and Forestville butter also form part of the display. Two small oval signs advertise Swift's Easter Festival radio program on March 21–23, 1931. (A. Hamm Coll., PIRP #7150.)

It is hard to imagine a Saint John hotel without a barbershop; as a Saint John newspaper wrote for the Dufferin in 1895, they had the "best tonsorial artists" in town. The Royal, Edward, Clifton, Admiral Beatty, and Victoria Hotels all had their own "tonsorial artists." The Victoria, at 85 King Street, is shown here c. 1912. The proprietors were Earl A. Kincade and Arthur G. Brown. Kincade barbered as far back as 1900 at the Royal Hotel, and Brown to 1909. (PIRP #4520.)

Raymond and Doherty's Royal opened in 1881. The guests of the Royal "carry away with them pleasant recollections of a high class house, with every convenience for the comfort of guests." The Royal prided itself on "Courtesy and the most painstaking attention to the comfort of guests." Memories of the Royal and its soda fountain provoke strong emotions, just as the mention of MRA's. Mitchell Franklin was the last owner of the Royal, c. 1973. (PIRP #2743.)

Market Square in 1923 was the site of several important Saint John businesses. Beginning at the left there are: Canada Permanent, Horton & Walsh, MRA's, the Union Bank of Canada, and the Mackay Lumber Company. Canada Permanent was built in 1912. Horton & Walsh, established in October 1847 by Henry Horton, operated at various locations until moving to 9 Market Square in 1923. Horton's closed on November 10, 1968. The buildings were demolished for the new city hall. (Horton Coll., PIRP #6033.)

SMT on King Street is shown here c. 1940. Also shown are Higgins Brother's Clothing and Charles Baillie's smoke shop. (Smith Coll., PIRP #4312.)

This 1942 photograph shows Robbins Drug Store on 17 Charlotte Street. Carl A. Robbins opened the store in 1939. Memories of Robbins include its scientific novelty, the "first magic eye door in Maritimes," the cosmetic counter, and its coffee shop and soda fountain under the direction of Victor Gustafsson. Perhaps Robbins was an early leader in the fast-food industry, for its motto was "fine food and fast friendly service." Shoppers Drug Mart took over the store in the 1970s. (Hamilton Coll., PIRP #6001.)

The head office of Wassons Pharmacy was at 9 Sydney Street. This August 1946 photograph includes a poster in the bottom right window advertising Norman Harris' orchestra, which performed at the Armoury on Saturday, August 10. Wassons moved from here to Courtenay Centre in 1966. (PIRP #4948.)

Margolian's Shoe Store was located at the corner of Union at Charlotte Streets, c. 1954. (PIRP #3885.)

City Market is shown in the above photograph on November 16, 1963. Dean's has been in the Market since 1876. In the 1942 photograph below, the Amherst Easter beef has just arrived from the annual Easter show. From left to right are: Harry Freestone, John Henderson, Abe Budavitch, Jack Murray, and Dave Gordon. (Gorman Coll., PIRP #3206; Dean's Coll., PIRP #7152.)

The Union Station opened in 1933. The interior was impressive "by reason of its surprising spaciousness." The combined concourse and waiting room was 40 feet high, ending in a "segmented arched plaster ceiling divided into bays by beams and panels." "The floors throughout are of terrazzo, in varying designs and colors. The walls of the concourse are lined to a height of several feet with ceramic tile of a brownish buff colour, relieved at the base and cap with lines of green and blue." It closed in June 1973, and was demolished by December of the same year. The top photograph dates to 1937, the celebration of King Edward VII's jubilee; the bottom one was taken on April 6, 1968. (PIRP #5194; R. Boudeau Coll., PIRP #4285.)

The demolition of Bassen's Clothing Store in 1968 ended 150 years of retail operations at Vernon's Corner (on King at Germain Street). Built in 1825 for tailor James Scouller, it was sold in 1833 to Moses Vernon, who lived on the second floor until 1868. Scovil, Fraser & Co., later renamed Scovil Bros. Co., were here until 1913 when they moved to the building next door. It was then remodelled for the Standard Bank, then Dominion Food, and in 1939, C.J. Bassen's clothing store. The Canada Permanent Trust Company built the present structure on the site. (Kilcup Coll., PIRP #6865.)

Many still lament the loss of MRA's and the Royal Hotel. MRA's, which opened in 1866 on Prince William Street, eventually included several buildings on King and around the corner on Germain, including the Wygoody building, which was built in 1895 and destroyed by fire in 1941. Although closed on January 1, 1974, memories of Winnifred Kean (shoes), Dickie Murphy (men's furnishings), the tea room, run by Ken Grass and later John Wedge, Don Kelly (shoes), Arnold Ogden (furniture), and the dozens of other employees, are still clear. The closing was described as a "letdown for everyone" and "like losing an old friend." (Edwards Coll., PIRP #4129; PIRP #4772.)

Eighteen
The Saint John General Hospital

Mayor W.W. White, M.D., lays the cornerstone of the Saint John General Hospital in August 1930. (Courtesy Region 2 Hospital Corp.)

The General Hospital, as viewed from Goodrich Street, c. 1951. (PIRP #635.)

The hospital in a 1959 photograph taken from Haymarket Square. (PIRP #2417.)